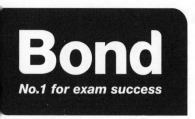

Bond
No.1 for exam success

No Nonsense
Maths

9–10 years

Contents

Lesson

Central pull-out pages

D1465234

OXFORD
UNIVERSITY PRESS

Recognising and ordering big numbers

MILLION	HUNDRED THOUSAND	TEN THOUSAND	THOUSANDS	HUNDREDS	TENS	UNIT
1	4	3	7	2	6	9

One million, four hundred and thirty-seven thousand, two hundred and sixty-nine

1. **Match the written number with the correct card. Join the dots.**

   a Six thousand four hundred and eighty-seven •

   b Fifty-nine thousand, eight hundred and seven •

   c Thirty-five thousand, two hundred and sixty-nine •

   d Seven hundred and eight thousand and three •

   e One million, one hundred and ten thousand and eleven •

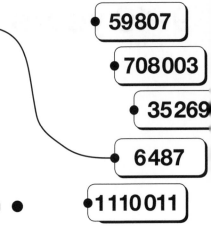

   59807

   708003

   35269

   6487

   1110011

2. **What number needs to go in the box?**

   a 28 717 = ☐ + 8000 + 700 + 10 + 7

   b 76 923 = 70000 + ☐ + 900 + 20 + 3

   c 83 641 = 80000 + 3000 + ☐ + 40 + 1

   d 52 876 = 50000 + 2000 + 800 + ☐ + 6

   e 39 681 = 30000 + 9000 + 600 + 80 + ☐

3. **Write these numbers as words.**

   a 7 623 _____

   b 223 400 _____

   c 78 231 _____

a Put these numbers in order, largest first.

| 2 369 | 223 693 | 26 393 | 93 362 | 6 932 |

| | | | | |

b Which two numbers have the digit 3 in the thousands column?

| | |

c Write the number 23 693 in words.

_____

Add the correct 'more than' (>) or 'less than' (<) sign.

a 4 837 ☐ 4 738   **b** 23 687 ☐ 23 678   **c** 286 383 ☐ 268 383

d 86 261 ☐ 86 621   **e** 31 002 ☐ 32 001   **f** 793 976 ☐ 793 796

How many more is ...

a 3 628 than 2 628? _1 000_   **b** 29 345 than 28 345? _____

c 326 516 than 326 416? _____   **d** 568 268 than 568 258? _____

				Total
Tough	OK	Got it!	**24**	24

Challenge yourself

a Using each digit only once, make the largest number you can. _____

| 2 | 9 | 6 | 8 | 5 | 3 |

b Write the answer for a in words. _____

_____

c Using each digit only once, make the smallest number you can. _____

d Add 10 000 to this number. _____

3

Negative numbers

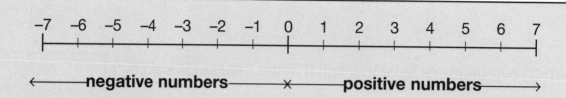

We use negative numbers to measure cold temperatures with a thermometer.

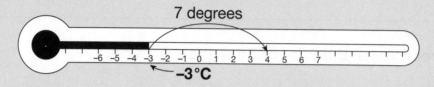

If the temperature rises from –3 °C to 4 °C the temperature has risen by 7 degrees.

1. By how many degrees does the temperature rise?

a The temperature is –1 °C. It rises to 8 °C. ___9___ degrees

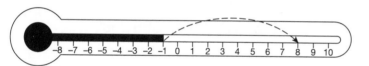

b The temperature is –5 °C. It rises to 4 °C. _____ degrees

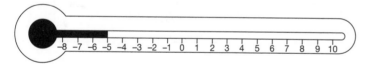

c The temperature is –3 °C. It rises to 10 °C. _____ degrees

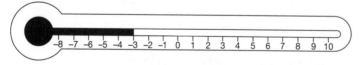

Try these without looking at a thermometer.

d The temperature is –2 °C. It rises to 7 °C. _____ degrees

e The temperature is –8 °C. It rises to 1 °C. _____ degrees

f The temperature is – 6 °C. It rises to 11 °C. _____ degrees

Answer these problems.

a The temperature is 2°C. It falls by 5°C.   What is the temperature now? _____

b The temperature is 6°C. It falls by 10°C.   What is the temperature now? _____

c The temperature is 12°C. It falls by 12°C.   What is the temperature now? _____

Put these numbers in order, lowest first.

a

| −1 | −4 | 0 | 4 | 1 |

_−4_ _____ _____ _____ _____

b

| 6 | −3 | 5 | −2 | 10 |

_____ _____ _____ _____ _____

c

| 2 | −2 | −12 | −22 | 12 |

_____ _____ _____ _____ _____

Tough	OK	Got it!	11

Total

11 / 11

Challenge yourself

Here are some rows of cards.
Fill in the missing cards so that the five numbers are in order.

a | −6 | _−5_ | −4 | _−3_ | −2 |

b | −1 | | 1 | | 3 |

c | −12 | | −10 | | −8 |

d | −3 | | −1 | | 1 |

e | −26 | | −24 | | −22 |

Addition and subtraction

This is how to do addition calculations using the 'carrying' method ...

```
  2 1 6 8        2 1 6 8        2 1 6 8        2 1 6 8
+ 3 9 5 3      + 3 9 5 3      + 3 9 5 3      + 3 9 5 3
─────────      ─────────      ─────────      ─────────
        1            2 1          1 2 1        6 1 2 1
─────────      ─────────      ─────────      ─────────
    1              1 1          1 1 1          1 1 1
```

When the numbers in a column total more than 10, the ten is carried to the next column.

1. **Complete these additions.**

   a   3 7 6 5   **b**   7 5 8 9   **c**   2 7 3 8
         + 1 6 9 7   + 1 6 6 3   + 3 3 8 5
         ─────────   ─────────   ─────────

         ─────────   ─────────   ─────────

   d   5 4 7 6   **e**   1 9 8 3   **f**   3 2 9 9
         + 3 7 6 1   + 1 5 6 1   + 1 7 1 6
         ─────────   ─────────   ─────────

         ─────────   ─────────   ─────────

   g   6 8 1 7   **h**   2 8 5 6   **i**   5 9 9 9
         + 1 6 6 6   + 3 7 7 5   + 2 8 8 8
         ─────────   ─────────   ─────────

         ─────────   ─────────   ─────────

2. **Find the total of ...**

   a 34 568, 128 and 4 458 _____

   b £0·78, £2·67 and £32·09 _____

   c 45·2, 530·78, 132·0 and 1·52 _____

   d 3·6 kg, 267 g, 23·67 kg and 5 g _____

QUICK TIP!
Remember to line up the units under units, tens under tens etc.

Do you remember how to do subtraction with bigger numbers?
If there are not enough units to take from, change a ten into 10 units.
If there are not enough tens to take from, change a hundred into 10 tens.

Look …

$$
\begin{array}{r}
3\,6\,7 \\
-\ 1\,6\,9 \\
\hline
\end{array}
\qquad
\begin{array}{r}
3\,\overset{5}{\cancel{6}}\,\overset{1}{7} \\
-\ 1\,6\,9 \\
\hline
8
\end{array}
\qquad
\begin{array}{r}
3\,\overset{5}{\cancel{6}}\,\overset{1}{7} \\
-\ 1\,6\,9 \\
\hline
8
\end{array}
\qquad
\begin{array}{r}
\overset{2}{\cancel{3}}\,\overset{15}{\cancel{6}}\,\overset{1}{7} \\
-\ 1\,6\,9 \\
\hline
9\,8
\end{array}
\qquad
\begin{array}{r}
\overset{2}{\cancel{3}}\,\overset{15}{\cancel{6}}\,\overset{1}{7} \\
-\ 1\,6\,9 \\
\hline
1\,9\,8
\end{array}
$$

Complete these subtractions.

a
$$
\begin{array}{r}
4\,7\,8 \\
-\ 1\,7\,3 \\
\hline
\\
\hline
\end{array}
$$

b
$$
\begin{array}{r}
2\,6\,0 \\
-\ 1\,8\,7 \\
\hline
\\
\hline
\end{array}
$$

c
$$
\begin{array}{r}
3\,9\,8 \\
-\ 1\,6\,7 \\
\hline
\\
\hline
\end{array}
$$

d
$$
\begin{array}{r}
5\,6\,8 \\
-\ 2\,2\,9 \\
\hline
\\
\hline
\end{array}
$$

e
$$
\begin{array}{r}
6\,7\,5 \\
-\ 2\,8\,8 \\
\hline
\\
\hline
\end{array}
$$

f
$$
\begin{array}{r}
3\,2\,9 \\
-\ 1\,9\,7 \\
\hline
\\
\hline
\end{array}
$$

Tough	OK	Got it!

19

Total

⟋ 19

Challenge yourself

Find the difference between …

a   8 253 and 517   _____

b   £3·28 and £1·75   _____

c   751·6 and 283·2   _____

d   3·3 litres and 230 ml   _____

QUICK TIP!
Again, remember to
line up the units under
units and tens under
tens etc.

Multiplying and dividing
by 10, 100 and 1000

When you **multiply** a number by **10**, the digits move **one place to the left**.
When you **divide** a number by **10**, the digits move **one place to the right**.

$$18 \times 1 = 18 \qquad\qquad 33 \div 1 = 33$$
$$18 \times 10 = 180 \qquad\qquad 33 \div 10 = 3{\cdot}3$$

When you **multiply** a number by **100**, the digits move **two places to the left**.
When you **divide** a number by **100**, the digits move **two places to the right**.

$$18 \times 1 = 18 \qquad\qquad 33 \div 1 = 33$$
$$18 \times 10 = 180 \qquad\qquad 33 \div 10 = 3{\cdot}3$$
$$18 \times 100 = 1800 \qquad\qquad 33 \div 100 = 0{\cdot}33$$

1. **Complete these number sentences.**

   a $38 \times 10 =$ _380_   **b** $168 \times 10 =$ _____

   c $560 \div 10 =$ _____   **d** $129 \times 100 =$ _____

   e $98 \times 100 =$ _____   **f** $11\,000 \div 100 =$ _____

   g $59 \times 10 =$ _____   **h** $1\,700 \times 10 =$ _____

   i $2\,400 \div 10 =$ _____   **j** $53\,800 \div 100 =$ _____

2. **Complete these number sentences.**
   Watch out, these include decimal numbers.

   a $26 \div 10 =$ _____   **b** $5{\cdot}23 \times 100 =$ _____

   c $59 \div 100 =$ _____   **d** $1.1 \times 10 =$ _____

   e $0{\cdot}238 \times 100 =$_____   **f** $41 \div 100 =$ _____

   g $1{\cdot}55 \times 10 =$ _____   **h** $1{\cdot}76 \div 10 =$ _____

   i $28 \div 10 =$ _____   **j** $500 \div 100 =$ _____

When you **multiply** a number by **1000**, the digits move **three places to the left**.
When you **divide** a number by **1000**, the digits move **three places to the right**.

18 × 1 = 18	33 ÷ 1 = 33
18 × 10 = 180	33 ÷ 10 = 3·3
18 × 100 = 1 800	33 ÷ 100 = 0·33
18 × 1 000 = 18 000	33 ÷ 1 000 = 0·033

Multiply and divide these numbers by 1 000.

a 54 × 1 000 = _____

b 516 × 1 000 = _____

c 240 ÷ 1 000 = _____

d 9·2 × 1 000 = _____

e 78·1 × 1 000 = _____

f 23 000 ÷ 1 000 = _____

g 123 × 1 000 = _____

h 760 × 1 000 = _____

i 200 ÷ 1 000 = _____

j 65 200 ÷ 1 000 = _____

k 44 × 1 000 = _____

l 1·1 × 1 000 = _____

m 7 ÷ 1 000 = _____

n 999 × 1 000 = _____

o 85 × 1 000 = _____

p 11 000 ÷ 1 000 = _____

q 0·002 × 1 000 = _____

r 17 ÷ 1 000 = _____

0

Tough   OK   Got it!   37

Total

/37

Challenge yourself

Answer these questions.

a Jason bought 21 bags of balloons for a big party.
There were 10 balloons in each bag.
How many balloons did he buy altogether? _____

b 2 400 paper clips fell on the floor when a piece of machinery broke in the paper clip factory. A box holds 100 paper clips. How many boxes of paper clips were lost? _____

c A book has 8 700 words on 100 pages.
If each page has the same number of words, how many words are on each page? _____

Times tables

If you cannot answer one of the times table questions straight away, carry on and come back to it when you have answered the other questions.

1. **How quickly can you answer these multiplication questions? Time yourself. Can you do them all in 90 seconds?**

$7 \times 6 =$ _____

$10 \times 8 =$ _____

$32 \div 4 =$ _____

$4 \times 4 =$ _____

$45 \div 9 =$ _____

$2 \times 8 =$ _____

$3 \times 7 =$ _____

$24 \div 6 =$ _____

$90 \div 10 =$ _____

$9 \times 6 =$ _____

$72 \div 9 =$ _____

$3 \times 4 =$ _____

$6 \div 3 =$ _____

$7 \times 4 =$ _____

$8 \times 8 =$ _____

$16 \div 4 =$ _____

$5 \times 5 =$ _____

$81 \div 9 =$ _____

$6 \times 3 =$ _____

$10 \div 5 =$ _____

$2 \times 4 =$ _____

$12 \times 3 =$ _____

$63 \div 7 =$ _____

$11 \times 3 =$ _____

$7 \times 7 =$ _____

$144 \div 12 =$ _____

$7 \times 1 =$ _____

$24 \div 3 =$ _____

$88 \div 11 =$ _____

$9 \times 12 =$ _____

$4 \times 8 =$ _____

$25 \div 5 =$ _____

$11 \times 12 =$ _____

$3 \times 9 =$ _____

$6 \times 5 =$ _____

$9 \times 9 =$ _____

$84 \div 7 =$ _____

$21 \div 3 =$ _____

$11 \times 5 =$ _____

$5 \times 3 =$ _____

$8 \times 6 =$ _____

$28 \div 4 =$ _____

$60 \div 12 =$ _____

$8 \times 3 =$ _____

$10 \times 10 =$ _____

How long did it take you? _____

Answer these questions.

a What are six sevens?

_____

b How many boxes (of 6 eggs) do 36 eggs fill?

_____

c What is 7 multiplied by 9?

_____

d 144 children went on a school trip.
   There were 12 children in each group.
   How many groups were there?

_____

e 6 children ate 4 biscuits each.
   How many biscuits did they eat in total?

_____

f What is seven times eight?

_____

g Divide 45 by 9.

_____

h 108 conkers were collected by 9 children.
   If each child collected the same amount,
   how many conkers did they each collect?

_____

i Share 63 equally between 9.

_____

j Multiply three by eight.

_____

| Tough | OK | Got it! | 55 |

Total

55

Fill in the boxes.

a $8 \times \boxed{} = 24$

b $\boxed{} \times 5 = 30$

c $6 \times \boxed{} = 24$

d $6 \times \boxed{} = 42$

e $8 \times \boxed{} = 88$

f $10 \times \boxed{} = 100$

g $21 \div \boxed{} = 7$

h $\boxed{} \times 7 = 49$

i $36 \div \boxed{} = 6$

j $18 \div \boxed{} = 3$

k $56 \div \boxed{} = 7$

l $\boxed{} \times 6 = 54$

Time

This timeline uses a 24-hour clock.

1:00 2:00 3:00 4:00 5:00 6:00 7:00 8:00 9:00 10:00 11:00 12:00 13:00 14:00 15:00 16:00 17:00 18:00 19:00 20:00 21:00 22:00 23:00 24:0

1.   Look at this bus timetable.

Bus stop	Pick-up time		
High Street	12:10	13:10	14:10
Church	12:20	13:20	14:20
Post Office	12:30	13:30	14:30
Sports centre	12:40	13:40	14:40

Answer these questions carefully.

a How many minutes are there between each stop? _____ minutes

b How many minutes does it take the bus to reach the post office after stopping at the

High Street? _____ minutes

c If you missed the bus at 12:30 outside the post office, what time would the next bus

be along? _____

d If you arrived at the church at 2:18, would you be just in time for a bus or too late? _____

e If you arrived at the sports centre at 12:40, how long would you be there if you

caught the 2:40 bus home? _____

f If you had finished shopping in the High Street at 1:13, what time would the

next bus be? _____

Fill in the gaps.

a 1 decade = _____ years

b 1 year = _____ months or _____ weeks or _____ days

c 1 week 3 days = _____ days

d 1 day = _____ hours

e 2 hours 20 minutes = _____ minutes

f 5 minutes 30 seconds = _____ seconds

Suggest the unit of time (for example minutes, days, years, etc.) that would be used for the following:

a to boil a kettle _____

b to walk across a road _____

c to grow from a baby into a 10-year-old _____

d to have a birthday party _____

e to fly to France _____

			Total
Tough	OK	Got it! **17**	17

Challenge yourself

Solve these problems.

a Titus got up at 08:10.
He left for school 40 minutes later.
His journey took 20 minutes.
School starts at 09:00.

Was Titus late? _____

If so, by how many minutes? _____

b The Chichester Colts football team kicked off at 14:30. They played 45 minutes each way and had a 15 minute break at half-time. At what time did the game finish? _____

(P.S. The Chichester Colts won 2–1!)

Length

1 kilometre (km) = 1000 metres
1 metre (m)   = 100 centimetres
1 centimetre (cm) = 10 millimetres (mm)

└──┘ 1 cm   ⊔⊔⊔⊔⊔⊔ 10 mm

1. **Underline the nearest correct measurement in each sentence. Do you think ...**

    a your table is   1 m,   2 m   or   30 m long?

    b this page is   5 cm,   15 cm   or   21 cm wide?

    c the ceiling is   3 m,   6 m   or   9 m high?

    d your pencil or pen is   1 mm,   7 mm   or   15 mm wide?

    e a house is   2 m,   4 m   or   15 m high?

2. **Which unit of measure would you use to measure ...**

    a your height?   _____

    b the length of a ship?   _____

    c the distance from Chichester to London?   _____

    d the width of a frisbee?   _____

    e the width of a paper clip?   _____

3. **Convert these measurements.**

    a 2 km = _____ m

    b 6·4 cm = _____ mm

    c $\frac{1}{2}$ km = _____ m

    d 3·2 m = _____ cm

    e 120 mm = _____ cm

What is the distance between the two arrows?

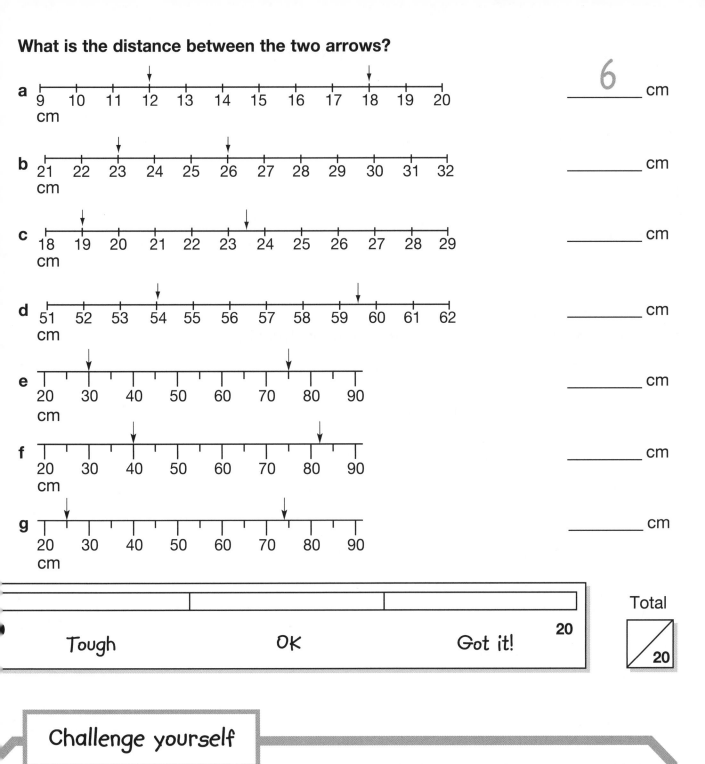

a ___6___ cm

b _____ cm

c _____ cm

d _____ cm

e _____ cm

f _____ cm

g _____ cm

| Tough | OK | Got it! | 20 |

Total

☐/20

Challenge yourself

Measure the length of these lines to the nearest mm. Write your answers in cm too.

a ___132___ mm ___13.2___ cm

b _____ mm _____ cm

c _____ mm _____ cm

d _____ mm _____ cm

Perimeter

The **perimeter** is the distance around the outside edge of a shape.

13 cm

12 cm

13 cm + 12 cm + 13 cm + 12 cm = 50 cm

The perimeter is 50 cm.
Opposite sides of a rectangle are the same length.

1. **Find the perimeter of each shape.**

17 cm

a 13 cm

17 cm + 13 cm + 17 cm + 13 cm = _____60_____ cr

25 cm

b 24 cm

= _____ cn

110 cm

c 15 cm

= _____ cn

2. **Measure the perimeters of these letters.**

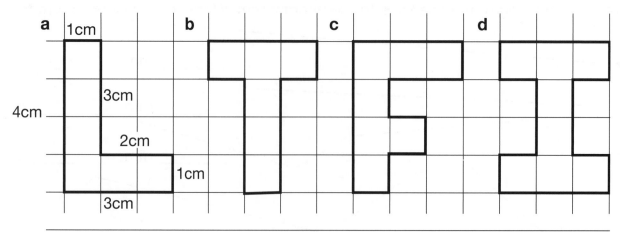

a 1cm   **b**   **c**   **d**

3cm

4cm

2cm

1cm

3cm

a _14_____ cm   b _____ cm   c _____ cm   d _____ cm

Use your knowledge of finding the perimeters of rectangles to solve the perimeters of these shapes.

a

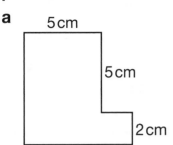

5 cm

5 cm

2 cm

7 cm

= _____ cm

b

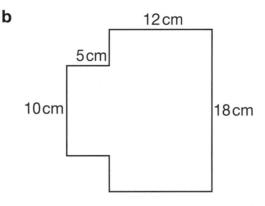

12 cm

5 cm

10 cm

18 cm

= _____ cm

What is the perimeter of ...

a the playground? _____ m

b the climbing frame? _____ m

c the netball court? _____ m

scale: 1 cm = 3 m

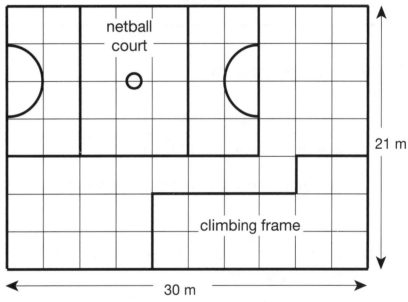

Parklands playground

netball court

climbing frame

21 m

30 m

Total

0

Tough   OK   Got it!   10

10

Challenge yourself

Solve these problems.

a The perimeter of a rectangle is 30 cm. The shortest side is 5 cm.
What is the length of the longer sides? _____ cm

b The perimeter of a rectangle is 42 cm. The shortest side is 6 cm.
What is the length of the longer sides? _____ cm

Which operation? +, −, ×, ÷

When considering a problem, it is not always easy to know which operation to use. Always read the problem carefully and try to visualise what it is asking.

It is also useful to remember the different terms that can be used in connection with each operation.

+	add	sum	total	altogether
−	take away	subtract	difference between	how many are left
×	times	multiply	product	multiplied by
÷	share	group	divide	divided into

1. Solve these problems.

a There are 6 eggs in each box.

How many eggs in 142 boxes? _____

How many boxes would 543 eggs fill? _____

b I think of a number and then subtract 116.
The answer is 142.

What was my number? _____

c Tuhil has 1 452 marbles.
Tina has half as many.

How many marbles does Tina have? _____

d In the school library there are 136 books on the top shelf.
There are 112 on the bottom shelf.
Caroline takes 32 books for a class project.

How many books are left? _____

e Mark started to read a book on Monday.
On Tuesday he read 10 more pages than on Monday.
He reached page 64.

How many pages did he read on Monday? _____

f I think of a number, subtract 12 and divide by 3.
The answer is 15.

What was the number? _____

Which operation sign goes in each box?

a 235 ☐ 69 = 304

b 520 ☐ 10 = 52

c 986 ☐ 235 = 751

d 56 ☐ 8 = 448

e 566 ☐ 245 = 321

f 38 ☐ 38 = 1 444

g 4 005 ☐ 45 = 89

h 254 ☐ 364 = 618

i 456 ☐ 3 = 1 368

j 786 ☐ 658 = 128

k 233 ☐ 13 = 3 029

l 132 ☐ 7 = 924

Tough	OK	Got it! **18**

Total

18

Challenge yourself

Look at questions 1b and 1f in this lesson.
Write two similar problems and test them on your friends or family.
(You need to work backwards!)

a I think of a number and then _____

The answer is _____

What was my number? _____

b I think of a number and then _____

The answer is _____

What was my number? _____

How am I doing?

1. **Write the missing numbers.**

   a 598 721 = _____ + 90 000 + 8 000 + 700 + 20 + 1

   b 36 542 = _____ + 6 000 + 500 + 40 + 2

   c 78 336 = 70 000 + _____ + 300 + 30 + 6

   d 58 061 = 50 000 + 8 000 + _____ + 60 + 1

   e 21 654 = 20 000 + 1 000 + 600 + _____ + 4

   f 92 835 = 90 000 + 2 000 + 800 + 30 + _____

2. **Put these numbers in order, lowest first.**

   a | 3 | | −3 | | 2 | | −2 | | 1 |

   ____ ____ ____ ____ ____

   b | 7 | | −17 | | −7 | | 0 | | 17 |

   ____ ____ ____ ____ ____

3. **Complete these calculations.**

a	**b**	**c**	**d**
4 5 7 8	2 2 8 9	5 8 2	6 6 4
+ 3 9 6 5	+ 3 4 8 8	− 1 4 9	− 5 3 9
_____	_____	_____	_____

4. **Find the answers.**

   a 41 × 10 = _____   **b** 460 ÷ 10 = _____   **c** 28 × 100 = _____

   d 3 700 ÷ 100 = _____   **e** 62 × 10 = _____   **f** 170 ÷ 10 = _____

   g 57 × 100 = _____   **h** 2 800 ÷ 100 = _____   **i** 39 × 10 = _____

   j 230 ÷ 10 = _____   **k** 49 × 1 000 = _____   **l** 21 000 ÷ 1 000 = _____

Fill in the gaps.

a 6 × _____ = 18

b 2 × _____ = 6

c 9 × _____ = 54

d 7 × _____ = 42

e _____ × 5 = 50

f 3 × _____ = 15

g 8 × _____ = 32

h _____ × 4 = 28

i 3 × _____ = 27

Complete.

a 2 hours = _____ minutes

b 240 seconds = _____ minutes

c 30 minutes = _____ seconds

What is the distance between the two arrows?

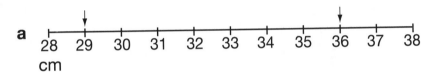

a
28   29   30   31   32   33   34   35   36   37   38
cm

_____ cm

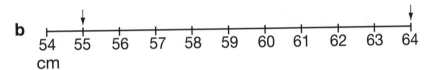

b
54   55   56   57   58   59   60   61   62   63   64
cm

_____ cm

Work out the perimeter of each shape.

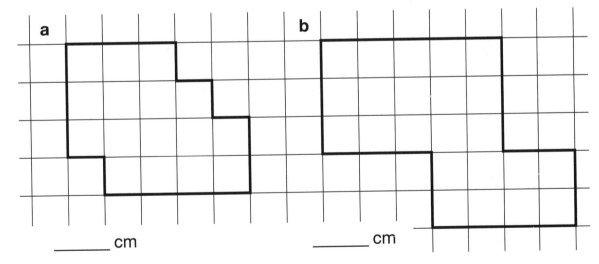

a

b

_____ cm   _____ cm

9. Which sign? +, −, ×, ÷

a 126 ☐ 361 = 487

b 272 ☐ 17 = 16

c 689 ☐ 98 = 591

d 34 ☐ 126 = 4 284

Total

44

21

Number bonds

$$72 + ? = 100$$

Adding numbers to 100 is easier than it looks.
First, in your head, the units need to add up to 10.

```
  72
+  8
————
   0
————
   1
```

Next, the tens need to add up to 10.

```
  72
+ 28
————
 100
————
   1
```

$$72 + 28 = 100$$

---

1. **Complete these number sentences.**

a $36 + \underline{\hspace{1cm}} = 100$ **b** $\underline{\hspace{1cm}} + 51 = 100$

c $79 + \underline{\hspace{1cm}} = 100$ **d** $\underline{\hspace{1cm}} + 97 = 100$

e $63 + \underline{\hspace{1cm}} = 100$ **f** $\underline{\hspace{1cm}} + 26 = 100$

g $25 + \underline{\hspace{1cm}} = 100$ **h** $\underline{\hspace{1cm}} + 86 = 100$

i $81 + \underline{\hspace{1cm}} = 100$ **j** $\underline{\hspace{1cm}} + 49 = 100$

k $\underline{\hspace{1cm}} + 56 = 100$ **l** $71 + \underline{\hspace{1cm}} = 100$

m $\underline{\hspace{1cm}} + 37 = 100$ **n** $32 + \underline{\hspace{1cm}} = 100$

o $\underline{\hspace{1cm}} + 11 = 100$ **p** $68 + \underline{\hspace{1cm}} = 100$

q $\underline{\hspace{1cm}} + 76 = 100$ **r** $57 + \underline{\hspace{1cm}} = 100$

How quickly can you do these?

a 10 + 10 = _____

b 12 + 12 = _____

c 15 + 15 = _____

d 7 + 7 = _____

e 21 + 21 = _____

f 17 + 17 = _____

g 11 + 11 = _____

h 14 + 14 = _____

i 230 + 230 = _____

j 310 + 310 = _____

k 260 + 260 = _____

l 190 + 190 = _____

m 250 + 250 = _____

n 380 + 380 = _____

o 470 + 470 = _____

p 290 + 290 = _____

Fill in the gaps. In each case, the two numbers need to be the same.

a 26 = _____ + _____

b 40 = _____ + _____

c 54 = _____ + _____

d 100 = _____ + _____

e 780 = _____ + _____

f 640 = _____ + _____

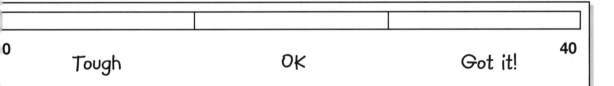

Tough   OK   Got it!

0   40

Total

40

Challenge yourself

Number bonds to 1000.

a 350 + _____ = 1000

b 490 + _____ = 1000

c 270 + _____ = 1000

d 135 + _____ = 1000

e 689 + _____ = 1000

f 551 + _____ = 1000

g 278 + _____ = 1000

h 984 + _____ = 1000

i 436 + _____ = 1000

Rounding numbers

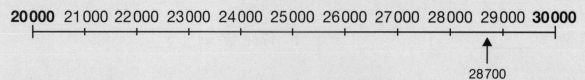

20 000 21 000 22 000 23 000 24 000 25 000 26 000 27 000 28 000 29 000 **30 000**

28 700

28 700 rounded to the nearest **thousand** is **29 000**.
28 700 rounded to the nearest ten thousand is **30 000**.

Rounding numbers can help you check your answers are close to the answer you are expecting.

1. **Fill in the gaps in the following sentences.**

    a **23 400** rounded to the nearest thousand is _____.

       23 400 rounded to the nearest ten thousand is _____.

    b **29 899** rounded to the nearest hundred is _____.

       29 899 rounded to the nearest ten thousand is _____.

    c **67 544** rounded to the nearest thousand is _____.

       67 544 rounded to the nearest ten thousand is _____.

    d **8 799** rounded to the nearest thousand is _____.

       8 799 rounded to the nearest ten thousand is _____.

    e **78 200** rounded to the nearest thousand is _____.

       78 200 rounded to the nearest ten thousand is _____.

    f **365 400** rounded to the nearest ten thousand is _____.

       365 400 rounded to the nearest hundred thousand is _____.

    g **999 999** rounded to the nearest ten thousand is _____.

       999 999 rounded to the nearest hundred thousand is _____.

Put a circle around the best approximation for the following.
Write the approximate answer for the number sentence.

a 34 670 + 45 899 = ? Approximate answer _____

34 000 + 46 000   35 000 + 45 000   35 000 + 46 000

b 123 997 + 3 124 = ? Approximate answer _____

124 000 + 3 000   123 000 + 4 000   123 000 + 3 000

c 98 698 – 32 999 = ? Approximate answer _____

97 000 – 30 000   98 000 – 33 000   99 000 – 33 000

d 134 134 – 97 654 = ? Approximate answer _____

134 000 – 97 000   135 000 – 98 000   134 000 – 98 000

e 999 999 + 555 555 = ? Approximate answer _____

900 000 + 500 000   900 000 + 600 000   1 000 000 + 600 000

Tough	OK	Got it!

0 ... **12**

Total

12 / 12

Challenge yourself

The following table shows the capacity of some stadiums.
Complete the table.

Stadium	Capacity	Nearest ten thousand	Nearest thousand	Nearest hundred	Nearest ten
Wembley	90 000				
White Hart Lane	36 230				
Millennium	72 500				
Old Trafford	75 811				
Emirates	60 361				
Anfield	45 522				
Stanford Bridge	41 837				
Murrayfield	67 800				

Multiplication

Look at these number sentences.

$$3 \times 4 = 12$$
$$3 \times 40 = 120$$

$$7 \times 6 = 42$$
$$70 \times 6 = 420$$

QUICK TIP!
Knowing this can help with long multiplication!

If a number in a number sentence is in the ten times table, the answer is also in the ten times table.

1. **Complete these number sentences.**

   a $5 \times 5 =$ _____

   $50 \times 5 =$ _____

   b $8 \times 4 =$ _____

   $8 \times 40 =$ _____

   c $9 \times 7 =$ _____

   $90 \times 7 =$ _____

   d $6 \times 3 =$ _____

   $6 \times 30 =$ _____

   e $4 \times 2 =$ _____

   $40 \times 2 =$ _____

   f $7 \times 6 =$ _____

   $7 \times 60 =$ _____

When you multiply a big number by a single digit you can lay it out like this:

	356		356		356		356
	$\times\ 6$		$\times\ 6$		$\times\ 6$		$\times\ 6$
	6		36		136		2 136
	3		3 3		2 3 3		2 3 3

2. **Complete these multiplications.**

   a   34
   $\times\ \ 3$
   _____

   b   45
   $\times\ \ 4$
   _____

   c   63
   $\times\ \ 5$
   _____

   d   623
   $\times\ \ 5$
   _____

   e   445
   $\times\ \ 8$
   _____

   f   923
   $\times\ \ 7$
   _____

g
$$725 \times 3$$

h
$$663 \times 6$$

i
$$523 \times 9$$

This shows you how to multiply a big number by a two-digit number using long multiplication:

```
    26
  × 6
  120
   36
  156
```

```
  1 3
  326
 × 15
 3260    (326 × 10)
 1630    (326 × 5)
 4890    (326 × 15)
```

a
$$232 \times 16$$

b
$$345 \times 18$$

c
$$331 \times 21$$

d
$$451 \times 32$$

e
$$226 \times 23$$

f
$$524 \times 19$$

Tough	OK	Got it!

21

Total

21

Challenge yourself

Solve these problems.

a Nanny Dawn had 16 grandchildren. She decided to give each of them £2·50.

How much money did Nanny Dawn give her grandchildren altogether? _____

b The Jolly family drove around Europe for three weeks. During the first two weeks they drove 1 232 miles each week. During the third week they drove 688 miles.

How many miles did they drive altogether? _____

Division

Remember, we can write a division calculation in different ways.

$195 \div 5 = 39$

$$5\overline{)195}\ \ (39)$$

We divide larger numbers like this:

First we ask how many 5s in 1 = 0

$$5\overline{)1\,9\,5}\ \ (0\ 1)$$

(We then carry the 1 to the next column.)

Then we ask how many 5s in 19
= 3 r 4

$$5\overline{)19\,^4 5}\ \ (3)$$

(We carry the 4 to the next column.)

Now we ask how many 5s in 45

= 9

$$5\overline{)19\,^4 5}\ \ (3\ 9)$$

QUICK TIP!
Line up the answer tens and units (above the line) with the tens and units (beneath the line).

1. **Divide the following.**

   a $4\overline{)7\,2}$

   b $6\overline{)9\,0}$

   c $3\overline{)5\,7}$

   d $7\overline{)1\,6\,1}$

   e $4\overline{)1\,2\,4}$

   f $5\overline{)3\,5\,5}$

2. **Find the answers to these number sentences.**
   Use the space provided to work out your answers.

   a $196 \div 2 =$ _____

   b $252 \div 7 =$ _____

   c $416 \div 8 =$ _____

   d $1800 \div 6 =$ _____

   e $2560 \div 5 =$ _____

   f $1107 \div 9 =$ _____

Divide the following.

Watch out, some of these division number sentences will have remainders!

a 77 ÷ 3 = _____ r ___

b 127 ÷ 6 = _____ r ___

c 130 ÷ 4 = _____ r ___

d 73 ÷ 2 = _____ r ___

e 2 525 ÷ 3 = _____ r ___

f 4 429 ÷ 7 = _____ r ___

For your workings

0   Tough   OK   Got it!   **18**

Total

18

Challenge yourself

Solve these problems.

a Moira Jackman bought a packet of sweets to share equally between her four children.

There are 166 sweets in the packet. How many sweets will each of her children get?

_____

Are there any sweets left over? If so, how many? _____

b Farmer Tom has 144 sheep. He divides them equally between six fields.

How many sheep does he have in each field? _____

The following week he buys another 12 sheep. If he also divides these sheep equally

between the fields, how many sheep will he now have in each field? _____

Calculations

There is always a way of checking a +, −, × or ÷ calculation.
Look at these number sentences.

$$38 + 71 = 109 \longrightarrow 109 - 71 = 38$$
$$268 - 126 = 142 \longrightarrow 126 + 142 = 268$$

1. Complete the second number sentence, by using the information in the first.

a $42 + 56 = 98$ $98 - \underline{56} = 42$

b $71 + 28 = 99$ $99 - 71 = \underline{}$

c $136 + 78 = 214$ $214 - 136 = \underline{}$

d $93 - 21 = 72$ $72 + 21 = \underline{}$

e $114 - 24 = 90$ $24 + \underline{} = 114$

f $236 + 84 = 320$ $320 - \underline{} = 236$

g $79 + 156 = 235$ $235 - \underline{} = 79$

h $387 - 189 = 198$ $198 + 189 = \underline{}$

Look at these number sentences.

$$27 \times 3 = 81 \longrightarrow 81 \div 3 = 27$$
$$216 \div 36 = 6 \longrightarrow 36 \times 6 = 216$$

2. Complete the second number sentence, by using the information in the first.

a $56 \times 3 = 168$ $168 \div 3 = \underline{56}$

b $186 \div 6 = 31$ $31 \times 6 = \underline{}$

c $702 \div 78 = 9$ $\underline{} \times 9 = 702$

d $29 \times 7 = 203$ $203 \div 29 =$ _____

e $96 \times 12 = 1\,152$ $1\,152 \div 12 =$ _____

f $448 \div 56 = 8$ $56 \times$ _____ $= 448$

g $432 \div 12 = 36$ $36 \times 12 =$ _____

h $78 \times 15 = 1\,170$ $1\,170 \div 15 =$ _____

. **Is the second number sentence in each pair right? Put a ✓ for right or ✗ for wrong.**

a $2\,187 + 1\,968 = 4\,155$ $4\,155 - 1\,968 = 2\,187$ ☐

b $28 \times 32 = 896$ $896 \div 29 = 32$ ☐

c $568 - 89 = 479$ $89 + 478 = 568$ ☐

d $5\,320 \div 266 = 20$ $266 \times 20 = 5\,320$ ☐

e $1\,876 + 549 = 2\,425$ $2\,425 - 549 = 1\,877$ ☐

f $459 \times 21 = 9\,639$ $9\,639 \div 21 = 458$ ☐

Tough	OK	Got it!

0   20

Total

/20

Challenge yourself

Complete the calculation pairs.

a $6\,888 \div 123 =$ _____ $12 \times 56 =$ _____

b   _____ $+ 589 = 1\,178$ $1\,178 -$ _____ $= 589$

c $78 \times$ _____ $= 38\,142$ _____ $\div 489 = 78$

d $4\,444 - 363 =$ _____   _____ $+ 4\,081 = 4\,444$

Angles

This is a right angle.

We measure angles in degrees (°)

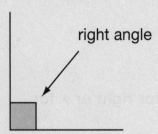

right angle

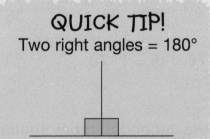
A right angle = 90°

If an angle is less than 90° it is called an **acute angle**.
If an angle is more than 90° it is called an **obtuse angle**.
If an angle is more than 180° it is called a **reflex angle**.

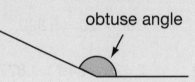

acute angle

obtuse angle

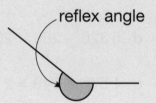

reflex angle

1. **Label the angles acute, obtuse, reflex or right angles.**

a

_____

b

_____

c

_____

d

_____

e

_____

f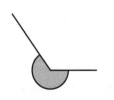

_____

2. **Mark the acute, obtuse, reflex and right angles, each in a different colour.**

a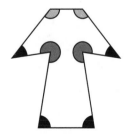

b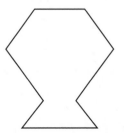

c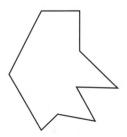

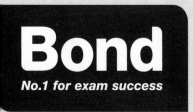

Bond
No.1 for exam success

No Nonsense
Maths

9–10 years

Parents' notes

What your child will learn from this book

Bond No Nonsense will help your child to understand and become more confident in their maths work. This book features all the main maths objectives covered by your child's class teacher during the school year. It provides clear, straightforward teaching and learning of the essentials in a rigorous, step-by-step way.

How you can help

Following a few simple guidelines will ensure that your child gets the best from this book:

- Explain that the book will help your child become confident in their maths work.
- If your child has difficulty reading the text on the page or understanding a question, do provide help.
- Provide scrap paper to give your child extra space for rough working.
- Encourage your child to complete all the exercises in a lesson. You can mark the work using this answer section. Your child can record their own impressions of the work using the 'How did I do?' feature.

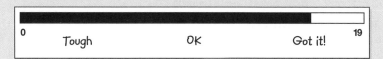

- The 'How am I doing?' sections provide a further review of progress.

Bond No Nonsense 9–10 years Answers

1 Recognising and ordering big numbers pp2–3

1 b 59807　c 35269　d 708003　e 1110011
2 a 20000　b 6000　c 600　d 70　e 1
3 a seven thousand, six hundred and twenty-three
　b two hundred and twenty-three thousand, four hundred
　c seventy-eight thousand, two hundred and thirty-one
4 a 223693 93362 26393 6932 2369　b 223693 93362
　c twenty-three thousand, six hundred and ninety-three
5 a >　b >　c >　d <　e <　f >
6 b 1000　c 100　d 10

Challenge yourself
a 986532
b nine hundred and eighty-six thousand, five hundred and thirty-two
c 235689　d 245689

2 Negative numbers pp4–5

1 b 9　c 13　d 9　e 9　f 17
2 a –3°C　b –4°C　c 0°C
3 a –4 –1 0 1 4　b –3 –2 5 6 10　c –22 –12 –2 2 12

Challenge yourself
b 0 2　c –11 –9 d –2 0　e –25 –23

3 Addition and subtraction pp6–7

1 a 5462　b 9252　c 6123　d 9237　e 3544
　f 5015　g 8483　h 6631　i 8887
2 a 39154　b £35·54　c 709·5　d 27·542 kg
3 a 305　b 73　c 231　d 339　e 387　f 132

Challenge yourself
a 7736　b £1·53　c 468·4　d 3·07 litres

4 Multiplying and dividing by 10, 100 and 1000 pp8–9

1 a 380　b 1680　c 56　d 12900　e 9800
　f 110　g 590　h 17000　i 240　j 538
2 a 2·6　b 523　c 0·59　d 11　e 23·8
　f 0·41　g 15·5　h 0·176　i 2·8　j 5
3 a 54000　b 516000　c 0·24　d 9200　e 78100
　f 23　g 123000　h 760000　i 0·2　j 65·2
　k 44000　l 1100　m 0·007　n 999000　o 85000
　p 11　q 2　r 0·017

Challenge yourself
a 210 balloons　b 24 boxes　c 87 words

5 Times tables pp10–11

1

42	4	32
80	25	5
8	9	132
16	18	27
5	2	30
16	8	81
21	36	12
4	9	7
9	33	55
54	49	15
8	12	48
12	7	7
2	8	5
28	8	24
64	108	100

2 a 42　b 6　c 63　d 12　e 24　f 56
　g 5　h 12　i 7　j 24

Challenge yourself
a 3　b 6　c 4　d 7　e 11　f 10　g 3　h 7　i 6
j 6　k 8　l 9

6 Time pp12–13

1 a 10　b 20　c 13:30　d in time
　e 2 hours　f 14:10
2 a 10 years　b 12 months or 52 weeks or 365 days
　c 10 days　d 24 hours　e 140 minutes　f 330 second
3 a minutes　b seconds　c years　d hours
　e hours

Challenge yourself
a Yes, 10 minutes　b 16:15

7 Length pp14–15

1 b 21 cm　c 3 m　d 7 mm　e 15 m
2 a cm or m　b m　c km　d cm　e mm
3 a 2000 m　b 64 mm　c 500 m　d 320 cm　e 12 cm
4 b 3 cm　c 4.5 cm　d 5.5 cm　e 45 cm　f 42 cm
　g 49 cm

Challenge yourself
b 95 mm 9.5 cm　c 135 mm 13.5 cm　d 160 mm 16 cm

8 Perimeter pp16–17

1 b 98 cm　c 250 cm
2 b 14 cm　c 16 cm　d 18 cm
3 a 28　b 70
4 a 102 m　b 54 m　c 66 m

Challenge yourself
a 10 cm　b 15 cm

9 Which operation? +, –, ×, ÷ pp18–19

1 a 852, 90½ boxes　b 258　c 726　d 216　e 27　f 5
2 a +　b ÷　c –　d ×　e –　f ×
　g ÷　h +　i ×　j –　k ×　l ×

Challenge yourself
Answers will vary

How am I doing? pp20–21

1 a 500000　b 30000　c 8000　d 0　e 50　f 5
2 a –3 –2 1 2 3　b –17 –7 0 7 17
3 a 8543　b 5777　c 433　d 125
4 a 410　b 46　c 2800　d 37　e 620　f 1
　g 5700　h 28　i 390　j 23　k 49000　l 2
5 a 3　b 3　c 6　d 6　e 10　f 5
　g 4　h 7　i 9
6 a 120 minutes　b 4 minutes　c 1800 second
7 a 7 cm　b 9 cm
8 a 18 cm　b 24 cm
9 a +　b ÷　c –　d ×

10 Number bonds pp22–23

1 a 64　b 49　c 21　d 3　e 37　f 74
　g 75　h 14　i 19　j 51　k 44　l 29
　m 63　n 68　o 89　p 32　q 24　r 43
2 a 20　b 24　c 30　d 14　e 42　f 34
　g 22　h 28　i 460　j 620 k 520　l 38
　m 500　n 760　o 940　p 580
3 a 13 + 13　b 20 + 20　c 27 + 27　d 50 + 50
　e 390 + 390　f 320 + 320

Challenge yourself
a 650　b 510　c 730　d 865 e 311　f 44
g 722　h 16　i 564

Rounding numbers pp24–25

a 23 000, 20 000   **b** 29 900, 30 000   **c** 68 000, 70 000
d 9000, 10 000   **e** 78 000, 80 000   **f** 370 000, 400 000
g 1 000 000, 1 000 000

a 35 000 + 46 000   Approximate answer 81 000
b 124 000 + 3000   Approximate answer 127 000
c 99 000 – 33 000   Approximate answer 66 000
d 134 000 – 98 000   Approximate answer 36 000
e 1 000 000 + 600 000   Approximate answer 1 600 000

Challenge yourself

Stadium	Capacity	Nearest ten thousand	Nearest thousand	Nearest hundred	Nearest ten
Wembley	90 000	90 000	90 000	90 000	90 000
White Hart Lane	36 230	40 000	36 000	36 200	36 230
Millennium	72 500	70 000	73 000	72 500	72 500
Old Trafford	75 811	80 000	76 000	75 800	75 810
Emirates	60 361	60 000	60 000	60 400	60 360
Anfield	45 522	50 000	46 000	45 500	45 520
Stanford Bridge	41 837	40 000	42 000	41 800	41 840
Murrayfield	67 800	70 000	68 000	67 800	67 800

Multiplication pp26–27

a 25, 250   **b** 32, 320   **c** 63, 630   **d** 18, 180   **e** 8, 80
f 42, 420

a 102   **b** 180   **c** 315   **d** 3115   **e** 3560
f 6461   **g** 2175   **h** 3978   **i** 4707

a 3712   **b** 6210   **c** 6951   **d** 14 432   **e** 5198
f 9956

Challenge yourself
£40·00   **b** 3152 miles

Division pp28–29

a 18   **b** 15   **c** 19   **d** 23   **e** 31   **f** 71
a 98   **b** 36   **c** 52   **d** 300   **e** 512   **f** 123
a 25 r2   **b** 21 r1   **c** 32 r2   **d** 36 r1   **e** 841 r2   **f** 632 r5

Challenge yourself
41, Yes, 2   **b** 24, 26

Calculations pp30–31

b 28   **c** 78   **d** 93   **e** 90   **f** 84   **g** 156   **h** 387
b 186   **c** 78   **d** 7   **e** 96   **f** 8   **g** 432   **h** 78
a ✓   **b** ✗   **c** ✗   **d** ✓   **e** ✗   **f** ✗

Challenge yourself
56, 6888   **b** 589, 589   **c** 489, 38 142   **d** 4081, 363

Angles pp32–33

a obtuse   **b** acute   **c** acute   **d** right angle
e obtuse   **f** reflex

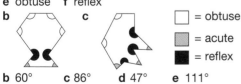

□ = obtuse
▨ = acute
■ = reflex

b 60°   **c** 86°   **d** 47°   **e** 111°

Challenge yourself
304°   **b** 225°   **c** 349°   **d** 105°   **e** 162°

Fractions pp34–35

a 5   **b** 2   **c** 8   **d** 6   **e** 5
f 7   **g** 21   **h** 9   **i** 5   **j** 9

b $\frac{1}{10}$ $\frac{1}{5}$ $\frac{1}{3}$ **c** $\frac{1}{6}$ $\frac{1}{4}$ $\frac{1}{3}$ **d** $\frac{2}{9}$ $\frac{1}{2}$ $\frac{3}{4}$ **e** $\frac{1}{5}$ $\frac{3}{10}$ $\frac{2}{3}$

f $\frac{1}{6}$ $\frac{1}{3}$ $\frac{2}{4}$ **g** $\frac{1}{6}$ $\frac{2}{10}$ $\frac{5}{9}$ **h** $\frac{1}{5}$ $\frac{1}{4}$ $\frac{3}{10}$

3 **a** $\frac{2}{5}$, e.g. $\frac{4}{10}$ **b** $\frac{1}{6}$ e.g. $\frac{2}{12}$ **c** $\frac{3}{4}$ e.g. $\frac{6}{8}$ **d** $\frac{3}{6}$ e.g. $\frac{1}{2}$
e $\frac{2}{8}$ e.g. $\frac{1}{4}$

4 **a** $\frac{2}{3}$ **b** $\frac{3}{4}$ or $\frac{6}{8}$ **c** $\frac{4}{10}$ **d** $\frac{1}{6}$ **e** $\frac{4}{12}$ or $\frac{1}{3}$
f $\frac{5}{8}$ **g** 1   **h** $1\frac{1}{4}$ **i** 2   **j** $\frac{3}{6}$ or $\frac{1}{2}$

Challenge yourself
a $\frac{1}{5}$ **b** $\frac{2}{7}$ **c** $\frac{3}{4}$ **d** $\frac{8}{10}$ or $\frac{4}{5}$

⑰ Mass pp36–37

1 **a** 3 kg   **b** 5 g   **c** 1 g   **d** 3 kg   **e** 80 g
2 **a** grams   **b** grams   **c** kilograms   **d** grams
    e grams   **f** kilograms
3 **a** 3000 g   **b** $\frac{1}{2}$ kg   **c** 2500 g   **d** $1\frac{1}{4}$ kg
4 **d** 65 kg   **e** 700 g   **f** 350 g
5 **b** 80 kg   **c** 20 kg

Challenge yourself
189 g flour   75 g fat   120 g sugar   3 tbsp treacle
$1\frac{1}{2}$ tsp ground ginger

⑱ Area pp38–39

1 **b** 14 cm²   **c** 40 cm²   **d** 3 cm × 6 cm = 18 cm²
    e 17 m × 7 m = 119 m²   **f** 15 m × 4 m = 60 m²
2 **a** 30 cm²   **b** 36 m²   **c** 56 cm²   **d** 90 m²

Challenge yourself
a 39 cm²   **b** 266 cm²

⑲ Shape pp40–41

1 **a** isosceles   **b** scalene   **c** right-angled
2 Answers will vary. The equilateral triangle should be the only
    regular polygon.
3 square or rectangle
4 Answers will vary   Examples: **a** cereal box   **b** dice
    c baked bean tin   **d** ball
5 **a** cube   **b** cuboid   **c** cylinder   **d** triangular prism

Challenge yourself

How am I doing? pp42–43

1 **a** 43   **b** 72   **c** 83   **d** 1
2 **a** 43 400   **b** 90 000   **c** 500 000
3 **a** 892   **b** 4780   **c** 4472
4 **a** 13   **b** 16   **c** 15 r1   **d** 96   **e** 98   **f** 56 r2
5 **a** 117   **b** 27   **c** 456   **d** 1 064
6 **a** 115°   **b** 70°
7 **a** 3   **b** 5   **c** 12   **d** 6   **e** 4   **f** 2
8 **a** 20 kg   **b** 700 g   **c** 30 kg
9 **a** 3 cm × 6 cm = 18 cm²   **b** 2 cm × 8 cm = 16 cm²
10 **a** Triangle should have two equal sides and two equal angles
     b Triangle should have no equal sides or angles

20 Number sequences pp44–45

1 a 7, 3, –1, –5 The numbers decrease 4 each time
  b 100, 109, 118, 127 The numbers increase 9 each time
  c 136, 151, 166, 181 The numbers increase 15 each time
  d 114, 107, 100, 93 The numbers decrease 7 each time
  e 44, 52, 60, 68 The numbers increase 8 each time

2 a

–7	–1	5	**11**	17	**23**	29	**35**	**41**	47	53

  b

303	**293**	283	**273**	263	**253**	243	233	**223**	**213**	203

  c

57	**66**	75	**84**	93	**102**	111	**120**	129	**138**	147

3 Red numbers: 7, 14, 21, 28, 35, 42, 49, 56, 63, 70, 77
  All numbers part of the 7 times table, multiples of 7, note pattern made.
  No, 100 would not be in the sequence.

Challenge yourself

a	4	8	12	16	20	24	28
b	8	16	24	32	40	48	56
c	12	24	36	48	60	72	84

8s are double 4s and 12s are 8s + 4s.

21 Problems with money pp46–47

1 a £53·44   b £36·50, £12·70, £18·90
  c £11·55   d £60506
  e Answers will vary
  f 10p, 20p, 26p, 30p, 36p, 46p, 52p, 62p, 72p, 78p, 82p, 88p, 98p, 108p

Challenge yourself
$7·20, €4·50

22 Percentages pp48–49

1 b 10% c 50% d 100% e 1% f 10% g 50%
  h 25% i 100% j 1%
2 b 50% c 6% d 50% e 70% f 89% g 46%
  h 100% i 23%
3 b 25% c 10%
4 Example a   b   c

Challenge yourself
b £10 c 70 cm d 20 books e 1p f £30 g £15
h 5 cm i 60 m

23 Multiples and factors pp50–51

1 b 15, 20, 50   c 16, 22, 10, 6 d 30, 90, 80
  e 18, 36, 54, 12 f 49, 77, 56   g 16, 36, 24
  h 24, 40, 56

2

Number	Factors	Factor pairs
8	1, 2, 4, 8	1 and 8, 2 and 4
9	1, 3, 9	1 and 9, 3 and 3
10	1, 2, 5, 10	1 and 10, 2 and 5
22	1, 2, 11, 22	1 and 22, 2 and 11
36	1, 2, 3, 4, 6, 9, 12, 18, 36	1 and 36, 2 and 18, 3 and 12, 4 and 9, 6 and 6

Challenge yourself

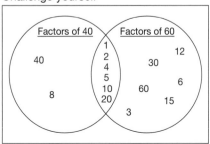

24 Square numbers pp52–53

1 b 4 c 5^2, 25 d 8^2, 64 e 10 × 10, 100 f 4 × 4,
2 9 16 25 36 49 64 81 100

Challenge yourself
a 1 b 8 c 27 d 64 e 125 f 216

25 Decimals pp54–55

1 b 12   c 14   d 18   e 21
2 c $19\frac{7}{10}$ d $36\frac{54}{100}$ e $67\frac{29}{100}$ f $59\frac{4}{10}$

3 a $2\frac{3}{4}$ b $4\frac{1}{2}$ c $6\frac{1}{4}$ d $3\frac{3}{4}$

Challenge yourself
2.1 $2\frac{1}{4}$ 2.3 $2\frac{1}{2}$ 2.6 2.8

26 Solving problems pp56–57

1 Yes
2 a 12   b 24
3 11, 13, 17, 19, 23, 29
  Each prime number is an odd number (apart from the prime number 2).
  When two prime numbers are added together the result is an even number (except when the prime number 2 is used
4 a CL b CLX c LXXVI d D e XII f LXXX

Challenge yourself
56 × 48 = 2 688 or 64 × 42

27 Capacity pp58–59

1 a 1 ml b 1 litre c 350 ml d 3 litres e 250 ml
2 a litres b ml c litres d litres
3 a 4 000 ml b 0.25 litres or $\frac{1}{4}$ litre c 500 ml d 3 litres
4 a 250 ml b 450 ml c 100 ml d 325 ml
  e 475 ml f 125 ml

Challenge yourself
a 12 b 20 litres

28 Line graphs pp60–61

1 a 6 am b 12 noon c 6°C d 1°C e 7°C
2

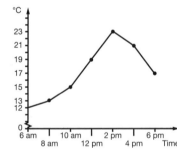

Challenge yourself
a 2 pm b 11°C c 19°C

How am I doing? pp62–63

1 a

28	35	42	**49**	**56**	63	**70**	77

  b

98	**86**	74	**62**	**50**	38	**26**	14

2 Example of workings:
  £4·50 × 3 = £13·50
  £13·50 + £12·99 = £26·49
  £50·00 – £26·49 = £23·51
  Jacob does not have enough money for the trainers, he only has £23·51 left.
3 a 50% b 50% c 100% d 20% e 25% f 80%
4 a 15, 50, 35 b 22, 18, 4 c 40, 90, 50 d 1, 2, 5, 1
  e 1, 2, 4, 8
5 a 4 b 16 c 25 d 100 e 49 f 9
6 a $15\frac{6}{10}$ b $12\frac{1}{10}$ c $9\frac{53}{100}$ d $11\frac{94}{100}$
7 a ml b litres c ml d litres

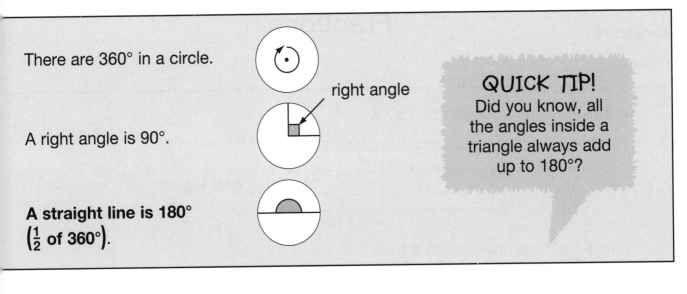

There are 360° in a circle.

A right angle is 90°.

right angle

QUICK TIP!
Did you know, all the angles inside a triangle always add up to 180°?

A straight line is 180° ($\frac{1}{2}$ of 360°).

Match the angles, so the two angles joined together will make a straight line (180°).

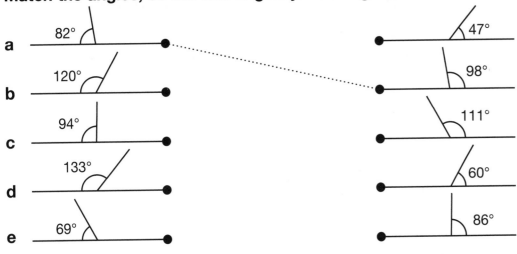

a 82°

b 120°

c 94°

d 133°

e 69°

47°

98°

111°

60°

86°

			Total
0 Tough	OK	Got it! 12	12/12

Challenge yourself

Calculate the missing angles.

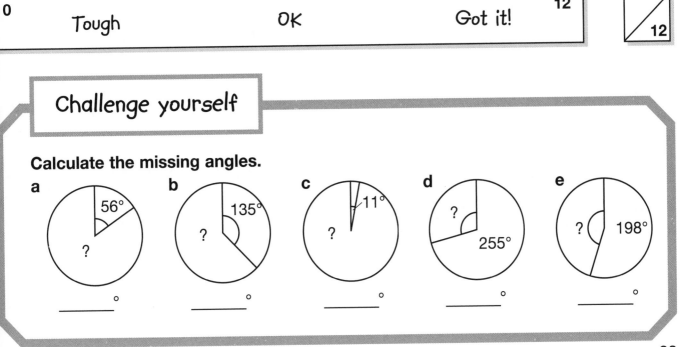

a 56° ?

b 135° ?

c 11° ?

d ? 255°

e ? 198°

_____ °   _____ °   _____ °   _____ °   _____ °

Fractions

To find $\frac{1}{2}$ of a number, divide it by **2**.

 $\frac{1}{2}$ of 6 = 3

To find $\frac{1}{5}$ of a number, divide it by **5**.

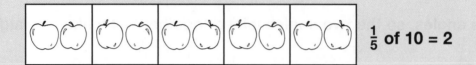 $\frac{1}{5}$ of 10 = 2

1. **What is ...**

   a $\frac{1}{2}$ of 10? _____

   b $\frac{1}{4}$ of 8? _____

   c $\frac{1}{3}$ of 24? _____

   d $\frac{1}{6}$ of 36? _____

   e $\frac{1}{4}$ of 20? _____

   f $\frac{1}{5}$ of 35? _____

   g $\frac{1}{2}$ of 42? _____

   h $\frac{1}{6}$ of 54? _____

   i $\frac{1}{5}$ of 25? _____

   j $\frac{1}{3}$ of 27? _____

2. **Place these fractions in order of size, smallest first.**

   a $\frac{1}{3}$ $\frac{1}{10}$ $\frac{1}{2}$ $\frac{1}{10}$ $\frac{1}{3}$ $\frac{1}{2}$

   b $\frac{1}{5}$ $\frac{1}{3}$ $\frac{1}{10}$ ___ ___ ___

   c $\frac{1}{6}$ $\frac{1}{3}$ $\frac{1}{4}$ ___ ___ ___

   d $\frac{1}{2}$ $\frac{2}{9}$ $\frac{3}{4}$ ___ ___ ___

   e $\frac{3}{10}$ $\frac{2}{3}$ $\frac{1}{5}$ ___ ___ ___

   f $\frac{1}{6}$ $\frac{2}{4}$ $\frac{1}{3}$ ___ ___ ___

   g $\frac{1}{6}$ $\frac{2}{10}$ $\frac{5}{9}$ ___ ___ ___

   h $\frac{1}{5}$ $\frac{3}{10}$ $\frac{1}{4}$ ___ ___ ___

Write the fraction shown in each picture then write an equivalent fraction for it.

a = _____   Equivalent fraction = _____

b = _____   Equivalent fraction = _____

c = _____   Equivalent fraction = _____

d = _____   Equivalent fraction = _____

e = _____   Equivalent fraction = _____

Complete the sums. Watch out, some of these are tricky.

a $\frac{1}{3} + \frac{1}{3} =$ _____

b $\frac{2}{4} + \frac{2}{8} =$ _____

c $\frac{2}{10} + \frac{1}{5} =$ _____

d $\frac{3}{6} - \frac{2}{6} =$ _____

e $\frac{9}{12} - \frac{5}{12} =$ _____

f $\frac{3}{4} - \frac{1}{8} =$ _____

g $\frac{1}{2} \times 2 =$ _____

h $\frac{1}{4} \times 5 =$ _____

i $\frac{1}{3} \times 6 =$ _____

j $\frac{1}{6} \times 3 =$ _____

Tough	OK		Got it! **32**

Total

/32

Challenge yourself

Find the answers.

a Daniel drank 200 ml. What fraction of a litre did he drink? _____

b What fraction of a week is the weekend? _____

c Callie was awake for 18 hours on Tuesday.

What fraction of the day was she awake for? _____

d Tom's house is 400 m from school. He walks to and from school each day.

What fraction of a km does he walk in one day? _____

35

Lesson 17

Mass

Mass = how heavy something is.

1 kilogram (kg) = 1000 grams **(g)**

grams ⟶

---

1. **Underline the correct mass for each sentence. Do you think ...**

   a a pet cat is approximately $\frac{1}{2}$ kg,   3 kg,   15 kg?

   b your pencil is approximately   5 g,   50 g,   500 g?

   c a sugar cube is approximately   1 g,   10 g,   100 g?

   d a bag of potatoes is approximately   3 kg,   100 kg,   300 kg?

   e a cup of flour is approximately   800 g,   80 g,   8 g?

2. **Which unit of mass would you use to measure ...**

   a a mouse? _____   **b** a letter? _____

   c a computer? _____   **d** a DVD case? _____

   e a T-shirt? _____   **f** a table? _____

3. **Convert these measurements.**

   a 3 kg = _____ g   **b** 500 g = _____ kg

   c 2.5 kg = _____ g   **d** 1250 g = _____ kg

Scales measure the weight of something.

What weight do these scales show?

a 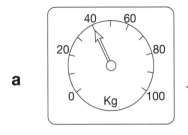 _40_ kg

b 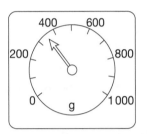 _____ kg

c 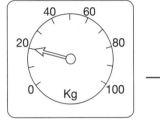 _____ kg

d _____ kg

e 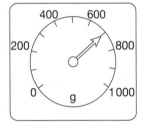 _____ g

f _____ g

Tough	OK	Got it!	20

0

Total

20

Challenge yourself

Change this ginger-biscuit recipe for 6 people to a recipe for 9 people.

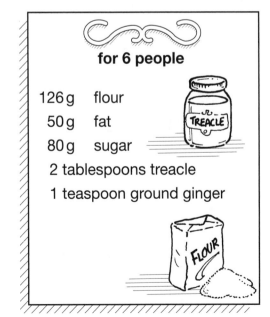

for 6 people

126 g flour
50 g fat
80 g sugar
2 tablespoons treacle
1 teaspoon ground ginger

for 9 people

____ g flour
____ g fat
____ g sugar
_____ tablespoons treacle
_____ teaspoon ground ginger

Area

Area is the space **inside** a 2D shape.
To find the area of this rectangle, use square centimetres (cm²).

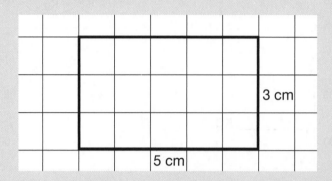

Count the number of squares inside the rectangle.
There are 15. The area is 15 cm².

You do not need to count the squares if you know how long the sides of the rectangle are.

Look carefully at the rectangle.
length × width = area
 5 cm × 3 cm = 15 cm²
The area is 15 cm².

1. **Find the area of each rectangle.**

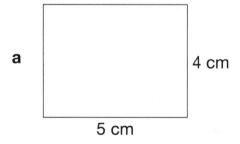

a   4 cm

 5 cm

= 5 cm × 4 cm = _**20**_ cm²

b   2 cm

 7 cm

= 7 cm × 2 cm = _____ cm²

c   4 cm

 10 cm

= 10 cm × 4 cm = _____ cm²

d 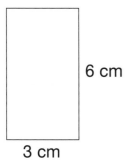 6 cm

3 cm

= _____ × _____ = _____ cm²

e  7 m

17 m

= _____ × _____ = _____ m²

f 4 m

15 m

= _____ × _____ = _____ m²

What is the area of a rectangle with …

a a length of 6 cm and width of 5 cm? _____ **b** a length of 9 m and width of 4 m? _____

c a length of 8 cm and width of 7 cm? _____ **d** a length of 10 m and width of 9 m? _____

Tough	OK	Got it! 9	

Total

9

Challenge yourself

Find the area of these irregular shapes.
Hint: Work out the area of the rectangles and add their totals together.

a
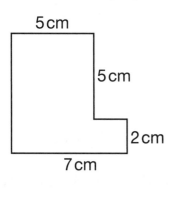
5 cm

5 cm

2 cm

7 cm

_____ cm²

b
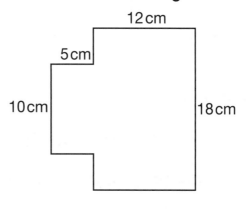
12 cm

5 cm

10 cm

18 cm

_____ cm²

Shape

Look carefully at these triangles.
Each triangle is slightly different.

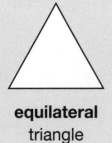 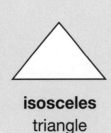 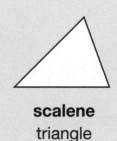 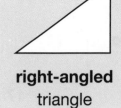

equilateral
triangle

isosceles
triangle

scalene
triangle

right-angled
triangle

1. **Answer these questions.**

   a Which triangle has two angles equal in size? _____

   b Which triangle has no two sides equal? _____

   c Which triangle always has a 90° angle? _____

2. **Cover the triangles at the top of the page.**

   Now draw your own triangles.
   Make each triangle slightly different to the one drawn at the top of the page.
   (*1 mark for each*)
   Label each triangle as either a regular or an irregular polygon.

equilateral triangle	isosceles triangle	scalene triangle	right-angled triangl

3. **Name this 2D shape.**

   The opposite sides of this shape are parallel and equal.
   The diagonals bisect one another and all four angles are equal.

   _____

Write an everyday object that is the same shape as these 3D shapes.

a cuboid _____

b cube _____

c cylinder _____

d sphere _____

The **net** of a 3D shape is ...
the 2D shape on paper that can be
cut out and made into the 3D shape.

Cereal

Cereal

Write down the 3D shapes these nets belong to.

a _____

b _____

c _____

d _____

			Total
Tough	OK	Got it! **14**	14

Challenge yourself

Draw eight nets of a cube. Each net must be different!

How am I doing?

1. Fill in the gaps.

a $57 + \rule{2cm}{0.4pt} = 100$

b $28 + \rule{2cm}{0.4pt} = 100$

c $\rule{2cm}{0.4pt} + 17 = 100$

d $99 + \rule{2cm}{0.4pt} = 100$

2. Fill in the gaps in the following sentences.

a 43 369 rounded to the nearest hundred is _____.

b 88 721 rounded to the nearest ten thousand is _____.

c 535 971 rounded to the nearest hundred thousand is _____.

3. Complete these multiplications.

a 223
× 4
_____

b 956
× 5
_____

c 172
× 26
_____

4. Divide the following.

a 4 ⟌ 5 2

b 6 ⟌ 9 6

c 5 ⟌ 7 6

d 6 ⟌ 5 7 6

e 3 ⟌ 2 9 4

f 7 ⟌ 3 9 4

5. Fill in the missing numbers.

a $117 - 34 = 83$ $83 + 34 = \rule{2cm}{0.4pt}$

b $27 \times 8 = 216$ $216 \div 8 = \rule{2cm}{0.4pt}$

c $365 + 456 = 821$ $821 - 365 = \rule{2cm}{0.4pt}$

d $1\,064 \div 56 = 19$ $56 \times 19 = \rule{2cm}{0.4pt}$

6. Fill in the missing angle:

a 65°   _____ °

b 110°   _____ °

What is ...

a $\frac{1}{3}$ of 9? _____

b $\frac{1}{5}$ of 25? _____

c $\frac{1}{2}$ of 24? _____

d $\frac{1}{10}$ of 60? _____

e $\frac{1}{4}$ of 16? _____

f $\frac{1}{6}$ of 12? _____

What weight do these scales show?

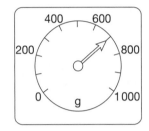

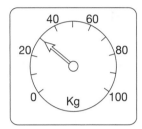

a _____ kg

b _____ g

c _____ kg

Find the area of each rectangle.

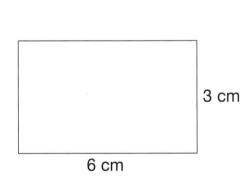

3 cm

6 cm

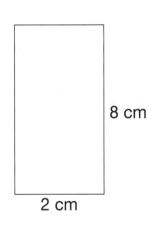

8 cm

2 cm

a _____ × _____ = _____ cm²

b _____ × _____ = _____ cm²

0. Draw these triangles.

a

isosceles triangle

b

scalene triangle

Total

35

Number sequences

Look at these number lines.
Rule: **the numbers decrease 6 at a time.**

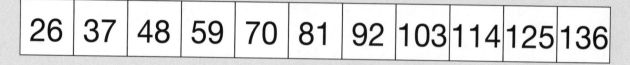

| 67 | 61 | 55 | 49 | 43 | 37 | 31 | 25 | 19 | 13 | 7 |

Rule: **the numbers increase 11 at a time.**

| 26 | 37 | 48 | 59 | 70 | 81 | 92 | 103 | 114 | 125 | 136 |

1. **Finish the number sequence and write the rule.**

a

| 35 | 31 | 27 | 23 | 19 | 15 | 11 | | | | |

Rule: _____

b

| 37 | 46 | 55 | 64 | 73 | 82 | 91 | | | | |

Rule: _____

c

| 31 | 46 | 61 | 76 | 91 | 106 | 121 | | | | |

Rule: _____

d

| 163 | 156 | 149 | 142 | 135 | 128 | 121 | | | | |

Rule: _____

e

| −12 | −4 | 4 | 12 | 20 | 28 | 36 | | | | |

Rule: _____

Fill in the gaps in these number lines.

a

| −7 | −1 | 5 | | 17 | | 29 | | | 47 | 53 |

b

| 303 | | 283 | | 263 | | | 233 | | | 203 |

c

| 57 | | 75 | | 93 | | 111 | | 129 | | 147 |

Count on in 7s from 0. Colour the numbers red.

What do you notice?

_____

_____

If you went on, would 100 be in your sequence?

_____

0	1	2	3	4	5	6	7	8
9	10	11	12	13	14	15	16	17
18	19	20	21	22	23	24	25	26
27	28	29	30	31	32	33	34	35
36	37	38	39	40	41	42	43	44
45	46	47	48	49	50	51	52	53
54	55	56	57	58	59	60	61	62
63	64	65	66	67	68	69	70	71
72	73	74	75	76	77	78	79	80

Tough   OK   Got it!   9

Total

9

Challenge yourself

Complete the table below by increasing the numbers in each row ...

a in 4s   **b** in 8s   **c** in 12s

a	4						
b	8						
c	12						

What do you notice?

_____

Problems with money

Often, without realising it, we solve problems with money.

When you choose a packet of sweets to buy, do you ever wonder if you have enough money left to buy a few more?

Before attempting a money problem, think carefully about the operation or operations (+, −, ×, ÷) you need to use to solve it.

1. **Solve the following problems.**

a Tuhil's mum bought him a pair of trousers that cost £15·99, a jumper for £12·50 and a new pair of shoes for £24·95.

How much money did she spend? _____

b What was the price of these items before the sale?

HALF PRICE SALE

Tennis racket
NOW
£18·25

Hockey sticks
NOW
£6·35

Football
NOW
£9·45

Tennis racket _____

Hockey stick _____

Football _____

c If a packet of stickers costs 55p, how much would 21 packets cost? _____

d Six people won £363 036 between them on the lottery.

How much did each person get? _____

e You have £1 worth of coins.
($4 \times 1p$, $3 \times 2p$, $4 \times 5p$, $3 \times 10p$, $2 \times 20p$)
Can you find at least ten different ways of using the coins to pay 45p exactly?

f You have three 26p stamps and three 10p stamps.
Find all the different amounts you could stick on a parcel.

Tough	OK	Got it!

0   6

Total

6

Challenge yourself

Converting to foreign currency.

The exchange rates for £1 are:

Bureau de change

A\$2·40
€1·50

A\$ = Australian dollars

€ = euros

QUICK TIP!
Exchange rate for £1 = how much foreign currency you would get for a pound.

How many dollars and euros do you get for £3?

dollars _____ euros _____

47

Percentages

Percentages are a way of dividing whole numbers into hundredths.

A percentage is the number of parts in every 100.

century = 100 years
per cent = in every 100
1 per cent = 1 in every 100
50 per cent = 50 in every 100

QUICK TIP!
% is the sign for **per cent**.

1 per cent can be written as $\frac{1}{100}$ or **1%**

50 per cent can be written as $\frac{50}{100}$ or **50%**

1. **Look at this table.**

Fraction	Decimal	Percentage
1	1·0	100%
$\frac{1}{2}$	0·5	50%
$\frac{1}{4}$	0·25	25%
$\frac{1}{10}$	0·1	10%
$\frac{1}{100}$	0·01	1%

QUICK TIP!
Don't forget to write the percentage sign.

Write the percentage that is the same as these fractions and decimals.

a $\frac{1}{4}$ = _25%_

b $\frac{1}{10}$ = _____

c 0.5 = _____

d 1 = _____

e $\frac{1}{100}$ = _____

f 0.1 = _____

g $\frac{1}{2}$ = _____

h 0.25 = _____

i 1.0 = _____

j 0.01 = _____

If $\frac{1}{10}$ = 10% $\frac{8}{10}$ = 8 × 10% = 80%

If $\frac{1}{4}$ = 25% $\frac{3}{4}$ = 3 × 25% = 75%

Write the percentages for the following fractions.

a $\frac{2}{10}$ = _20%_

b $\frac{1}{2}$ = _____

c $\frac{6}{100}$ = _____

d $\frac{2}{4}$ = _____

e $\frac{7}{10}$ = _____

f $\frac{89}{100}$ = _____

g $\frac{46}{100}$ = _____

h $\frac{2}{2}$ = _____

i $\frac{23}{100}$ = _____

What percentage of the shape below is shaded?

a _50%_

b _____

c _____

Colour in the correct percentage on these shapes.

a 20%

b 75%

c 70%

Tough	OK	Got it!

22

Total

22

Challenge yourself

Find ...

a 50% of £100 = _£50_

b 10% of £100 = _____

c 70% of 100 cm = _____

d 20% of 100 books = _____

e 1% of 100p = _____

f 50% of £60 = _____

g 25% of £60 = _____

h 10% of 50 cm = _____

i 75% of 80 m = _____

Multiples and factors

A **multiple** is a number that can be divided **exactly** by a smaller number.

30, 15, 10, 25, 45 are all multiples of **5**.

All these numbers divide exactly by 5.

1. **Ring the numbers in the box that are multiples of**

a 3 | 8 | (18) | 25 | (30) | (24) | 5 | (21)

b 5 | 15 | 18 | 32 | 20 | 43 | 7 | 50

c 2 | 27 | 16 | 33 | 22 | 19 | 10 | 6

d 10 | 69 | 30 | 45 | 90 | 38 | 80 | 21

e 6 | 59 | 18 | 61 | 36 | 21 | 54 | 12

f 7 | 38 | 49 | 77 | 9 | 22 | 39 | 56

g 4 | 9 | 55 | 37 | 29 | 16 | 36 | 24

h 8 | 67 | 24 | 40 | 19 | 56 | 79 | 25

A **factor** is a number that can be divided **exactly** into a bigger number.

15 has 4 numbers that divide equally into it.

1, **3**, **5** and **15** are factors of **15**.

15 has 4 factors.

The **factor pairs** of 15 are

1 and 15 (as 1 × 15 = 15)

3 and 5 (as 3 × 5 = 15)

First list the factors then list the factor pairs of these numbers. *(5 marks)*

Number	Factors	Factor pairs
8		
9		
10		
22		
36		

Tough   OK   Got it!   **12**

Total

Challenge yourself

Complete this Venn diagram to find the factors common to both 40 and 60.

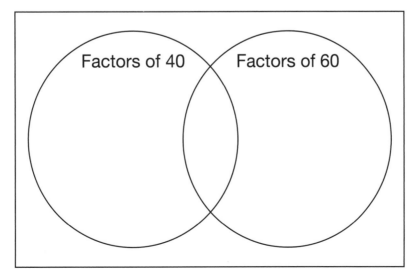

Square numbers

The square of a number is the number multiplied by itself.
Write the calculation like this ... $3^2 = 9$

$$3 \quad \times \quad 3 \quad = \quad 9$$

$$3 \quad 3 \quad 3 \quad = \quad 9$$

Look!
When the answer is drawn it looks like a square.

1. **Fill in the gaps.**

a $6 \times 6 = 6^2 =$ _____ = **36**

b $2 \times 2 = 2^2 =$ _____ = _____

c $5 \times 5 =$ _____ = _____ = _____

d $8 \times 8 =$ _____ = _____ = _____

e _____ $\times$ _____ $= 10^2 =$ _____ = _____

f _____ $\times$ _____ $= 4^2 =$ _____ = _____

Answer the following.

1^2 = ___1___

2^2 = ___4___

3^2 = _____

4^2 = _____

5^2 = _____

6^2 = _____

7^2 = _____

8^2 = _____

9^2 = _____

10^2 = _____

Use this space to continue drawing the squares in order. Draw a square around the shape.

Tough	OK	Got it!	6

Total

6

Challenge yourself

When a number is multiplied by itself and then by itself again it is known as a cube number. The calculation is written like this ...

$3^3 = 3 \times 3 \times 3 = 27$

Find these cube numbers.

a $1^3 = 1 \times 1 \times 1 =$ _____

b $2^3 = 2 \times 2 \times 2 =$ _____

c $3^3 = 3 \times 3 \times 3 =$ _____

d $4^3 = 4 \times 4 \times 4 =$ _____

e $5^3 = 5 \times 5 \times 5 =$ _____

f $6^3 = 6 \times 6 \times 6 =$ _____

Decimals

In decimals, the **decimal point** (·) separates the whole numbers from the numbers that are less than 1. Everything before the decimal point is a whole number. Everything after it is a fraction.

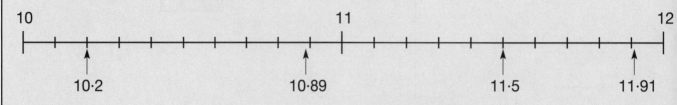

Look at the arrows and decimals written below the number line.

10·2 is equivalent to 10 whole numbers and **2 tenths**.
11·91 is equivalent to 11 whole numbers and **91 hundredths**.

1. **Round to the nearest whole number.**

 a 10·15 rounded to the nearest whole number is ___10___.

 b 12·32 rounded to the nearest whole number is _____.

 c 13·9 rounded to the nearest whole number is _____.

 d 17·6 rounded to the nearest whole number is _____.

 e 21·23 rounded to the nearest whole number is _____.

15 whole numbers and 3 tenths
15·3 can also be written as a **mixed number** $15\frac{3}{10}$

16 whole numbers and 57 hundredths
16·57 can also be written as a mixed number $16\frac{57}{10\bullet}$

2. **Write each of these decimal numbers as a mixed number.**

 a 16·81 = ___$16\frac{81}{100}$___

 b 21·36 = ___$21\frac{36}{100}$___

 c 19·7 = _____

 d 36·54 = _____

 e 67·29 = _____

 f 59·4 = _____

Do you remember?

$\frac{5}{10}$ is the same as $\frac{1}{2}$ $\frac{5}{10} = \frac{1}{2}$

So $2.5 = 2\frac{1}{2}$

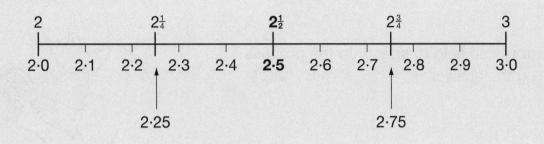

Match the equivalent numbers with a line.

a 2·75 ●   ● $6\frac{1}{4}$

b 4·5 ●   ● $2\frac{3}{4}$

c 6·25 ●   ● $3\frac{3}{4}$

d 3·75 ●   ● $4\frac{1}{2}$

Tough	OK	Got it!

12

Total

12

Write these numbers in order, smallest first.

2.1 2.3 $2\frac{1}{2}$ 2.8 $2\frac{1}{4}$ 2.6

2.1 ___ ___ ___ ___ ___

Solving problems

Solving problems in maths is a way of playing with numbers.
Approach each problem as a challenge!

Calculators can help to speed up the process
of finding the answer.

1. Is it true that the product of any two consecutive numbers is even? _____

For your workings

2. 2 squares can make 1 rectangle,

and 4 squares can make 2 different rectangles.

a How many squares are needed to make three different rectangles? _____

b How many squares are needed to make four different rectangles? _____

A prime number is a number that can only be divided by 1 and itself.

a Write all of the prime numbers between 10 and 30.

____ ____ ____ ____ ____ ____

b What do all of the prime numbers you have written have in common?

_____

c When you add together any two of the prime numbers you have written, what do you notice?

_____

Solve these roman numeral number sentences.
Write your answers in roman numerals!

a C + L = _____

b C + LX = _____

c XC − XIV = _____

d M − D = _____

e XX − VIII = _____

f XL + XL = _____

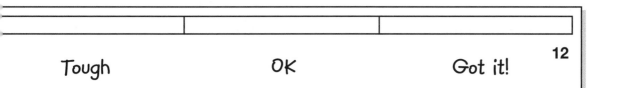

Tough	OK	Got it!	**12**

Total

12

Challenge yourself

Each  represents a missing digit. They can be different numbers.

Use a calculator to help you complete the number sentence.

$$\triangle\triangle \times \boxed{4}\triangle = 2\,688$$

Capacity

Capacity = the amount of space inside something

 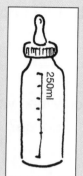

1 litre **(l)** = 1000 millilitres **(ml)**

1. **Underline the correct capacity for each sentence. Do you think ...**

   a a raindrop is approximately   1 ml,   100 ml,   500 ml?

   b a carton of milk is approximately   1 litre,   10 litres, 100 litres?

   c a mug is approximately   35 ml,   350 ml,   3 500 ml?

   d a family-sized ice-cream tub is approximately   0.3 litres, 3 litres,   30 litres?

   e a jam jar is approximately   2 ml,   25 ml,   250 ml?

2. **Which unit would you use to measure ...**

   a the capacity of a bath? _____

   b the capacity of an egg cup? _____

   c a bottle of lemonade? _____

   d the capacity of a fish tank? _____

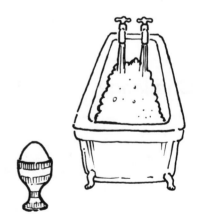

3. **Convert these measurements.**

   a 4 litres = _____ ml   **b** 250 ml = _____ litres

   c 0.5 litres = _____ ml   **d** 3 000 ml = _____ litres

Cylinders with millilitres marked on the side can be used to measure capacity. Read the capacities below.

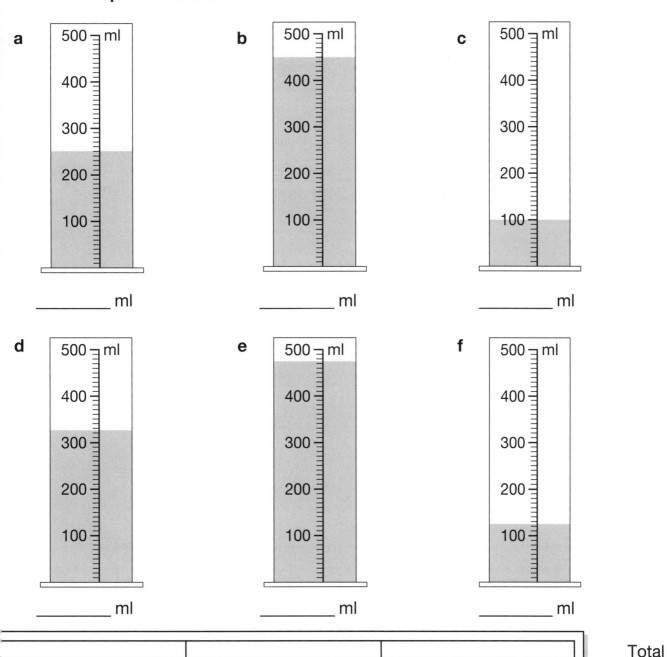

a   _____ ml

b   _____ ml

c   _____ ml

d   _____ ml

e   _____ ml

f   _____ ml

Tough	OK	Got it!

Total

19

19

Challenge yourself

Solve these problems.

a   Dad makes 3 litres of soup on Bonfire night. One cup of soup holds 250 ml. How many people can have a cup of soup? _____

b   A car is filled with 20 000 millilitres of petrol. How many litres is this? _____

Line graphs

A **line graph** shows information in a simple way.

The line graph below shows the temperature outside on a day in January.

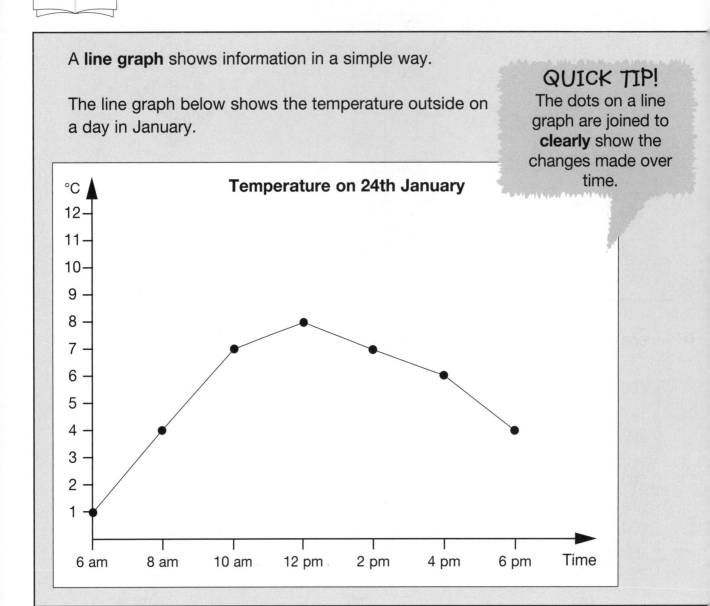

Temperature on 24th January

1. **Look at the line graph and answer the following questions.**

   a At what time was the temperature 1 °C? _____

   b At what time was the temperature at its highest point? _____

   c What is the temperature at 4 pm? _____

   d How much did the temperature drop between 12 noon and 2 pm? _____

   e How many degrees did the temperature rise from 6 am to 12 noon? _____

Draw a line graph showing the following information.

Remember to join the dots. *(8 marks: 1 per dot, 1 for line)*

The temperature on 31st July							
Time	6 am	8 am	10 am	12 noon	2 pm	4 pm	6 pm
°C	12	13	15	19	23	21	17

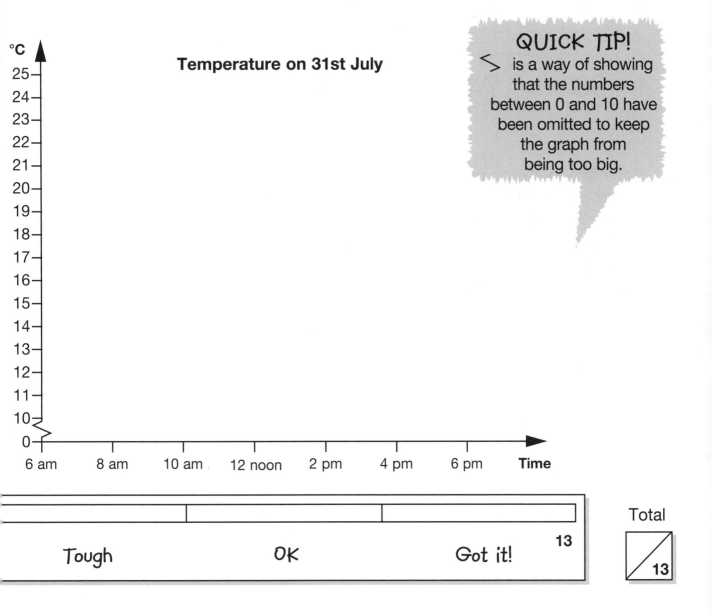

Temperature on 31st July

QUICK TIP!

⌇ is a way of showing that the numbers between 0 and 10 have been omitted to keep the graph from being too big.

			Total
Tough	OK	Got it! **13**	13

Challenge yourself

Use the graph you have drawn to answer the following questions.

a What was the hottest time of the day? _____

b How many degrees did the temperature rise between 6 am and 2 pm? _____

c What was the temperature at 12 noon? _____

How am I doing?

1. **Fill in the gaps in the number lines.**

a
28		42			63		77

b
98		74			38		14

2. **Solve the following problem.**

Jacob was given £50 for his birthday. He spent £12·99 on a DVD and bought three albums from iTunes for £4·50 each.

He then found a pair of trainers he wanted to buy for £25·00. Did he have enough money left to buy them? _____

How much money did he have left? _____

For your workings

3. **Fill in the missing percentages.**

a $\frac{1}{2}$ = _____ %

b 0·5 = _____ %

c 1 = _____ %

d $\frac{1}{5}$ = _____ %

e 0·25 = _____ %

f $\frac{4}{5}$ = _____ %

Ring the numbers in the box that are multiples of ...

a 5

| 21 | 36 | 15 | 46 | 50 | 35 | 6 |

b 2

| 13 | 22 | 37 | 18 | 7 | 4 | 9 |

c 10

| 18 | 40 | 31 | 90 | 28 | 64 | 50 |

List the factors for these numbers.

d 10

_____ _____ _____ _____

e 8

_____ _____ _____ _____

Work out the following square numbers.

a 2^2 = _____

b 4^2 = _____

c 5^2 = _____

d 10^2 = _____

e 7^2 = _____

f 3^2 = _____

Write these numbers as fractions.

a 15·6 = 15 $\frac{}{10}$

b 12·1 = _____

c 9·53 = _____

d 11·94 = _____

Which unit, litres or millilitres, would you use to measure the capacity of a ...

a mug? _____

b bucket? _____

c baby bottle? _____

d paddling pool? _____

Total

28

Try the 10–11 years book

Lesson 1	**Numbers and place value**

ten million	million	hundred thousand	ten thousand	thousands	hundreds	tens	units
1	**0**	**0**	**0**	**0**	**0**	**0**	**0**

Ten million

1. **Write the written number in numerals.**

   a six million, thirty-eight thousand and two _____

   b nine million, one hundred thousand and fifty-five _____

   c three million, five hundred and seventy-seven thousand and eleven _____

   d five million, eight hundred and one thousand, three hundred and sixty _____

   e nine million, nine hundred and ninety-nine thousand, nine hundred and nine _____

2. **What number needs to go in the box?**

   a $2\,678\,450 = 2\,000\,000 + 600\,000 +$ _____ $+ 8\,000 + 400 + 50 + 0$

   b $8\,878\,676 = 8\,000\,000 + 800\,000 + 70\,000 +$ _____ $+ 600 + 70 + 6$

   c $3\,585\,732 =$ _____ $+ 500\,000 + 80\,000 + 5\,000 + 700 + 30 + 2$

   d $9\,999\,999 = 9\,000\,000 + 900\,000 +$ _____ $+ 9\,000 + 900 + 90 + 9$

   e $1\,213\,141 = 1\,000\,000 + 200\,000 + 10\,000 + 3\,000 +$ _____ $+ 40 + 1$

3. **Write these numbers as words.**

   a $4\,323\,675$ _____

   b $308\,004$ _____

   c $7\,004\,399$ _____

64